William Standish

The argument of Wm. H. Standish before Congress

Explaining the Beaubien title in the lake front lands at Chicago

William Standish

The argument of Wm. H. Standish before Congress
Explaining the Beaubien title in the lake front lands at Chicago

ISBN/EAN: 9783337149246

Printed in Europe, USA, Canada, Australia, Japan

Cover: Foto ©ninafisch / pixelio.de

More available books at **www.hansebooks.com**

THE ARGUMENT

OF

WM. H. STANDISH

BEFORE CONGRESS,

EXPLAINING

The Beaubien Title in the Lake Front Lands at Chicago, in Section 10,

WITH REASONS

Why They Should be Granted to the Beaubiens by Congress,

And not Donated to Chicago,

With Appendix Containing Proofs.

WASHINGTON, D. C.:

R. BERESFORD, PRINTER, 523 SEVENTH ST., N. W.,

1878.

The Argument of WM. H. STANDISH *before Congress, explaining the* BEAUBIEN *title in the Lake Front Lands at Chicago, in section* 10, *with reasons why they should be granted to the* BEAUBIENS *by Congress, and not donated to Chicago.*

This land, being described in Senate bill 773, and the same land described in Representative Harrison's Lake Front bill in the House, was ceded by the Indians, August 3, 1795, at the treaty of Greenville. It was not entered as a reservation until 1824, and from August, 1812, to July, 1816, was not a post of any kind, and had no buildings on of the Government, or soldiers or agents of the Government in possession; hence, between these last dates the land was vacant and unappropriated, and susceptible of passing in equity under the pre-emption and other land laws out of the United States.

1st Attorney Generals Opinions, 292. .

6th McLean, 517, U. S. *vs.* R. R. Bridge Co.

15th Peters, 407, U. S. *vs.* Fitzgerald.

To explain: when troops stop and camp on public land, without having it entered in the Land Office, it remains appropriated until they pass on, whether their stay is long or short. After it has been entered as reserved in the Land Office, they must not only move on, but the entry made must be canceled; both these things then need to concur, when the land falls back into its original condition, controlled by the general land laws for disposition.

Second. Between these dates two pre-emption laws were passed, by which all of the equitable title during that time did pass out of the United States and become vested in Jean B. Beaubien, the father of these claimants.

The first of these acts was made February 15, 1813. (2 vol. Stat., 797.)

An amendment to this law was made April 29, 1816. (3d vol. Stat., page 554.)

Third. The following affidavits show that Beaubien had done more than to have purchased an early settlement claim on this land, and not to have removed from the then Illinois Territory, which was all that was required by this law to be a vested, equitable owner of the land. The affidavits referred to are those of Colonel E. D. Taylor, who is certified to by Representative Morrison, of that State; Madore B. Beaubien, who is certified to by Representative Ryan, of Topeka, Kansas; also, those of John B. Letendre, David McKee, Mr. LeVassar, all credible persons.

The evident reason why continued residence on the land was not made necessary by this law, or something near continued residence on it, was because this law was passed when we were at war, and having much trouble with the Indians of Illinois Territory, and it could not be clearly foreseen what the exigencies of the settlers of that territory might be. It was deemed prudent to give them and their families liberty to live where they might deem it most expedient and safe until their lands should come into market, and so this law was made accordingly.

In the case of Bird *vs.* Cravens *et al.*, 1st Mo., 282, the purchaser of one of these unentered rights left the land; his whereabouts was unknown, and the person he had purchased it from entered the tract in his own name, and got the patent title, and was held a trustee of it for the absent settler he had previously sold his unentered right to.

The act of April 29, 1816, also authorized a settler before survey to take any uninclosed unappropriated land, in any fractional quarter section in and around his buildings and improvements he might then have on the land, and to authorize the register and receiver to so divide the land when it would come by him to be entered at the Land Office.

None of the land south of Randolph street, in this tract, which is this land, was reserved, or in the use of the post, prior to October 1, 1824, and this was true of nearly all the land in this fractional quarter section. The Government field spoken of in the Wolcott letter, in 13th Peters, 498, was not in this fractional quarter section, but west of State street, in section nine. (See affidavit of Madore B. Beaubien.) These laws were not limited in the time they should last, like the 1830, 1834, and 1838 laws. They were to stand until repealed. They have never been repealed. They were not affected by the law of 1841, and are no part of that act. That act and these acts apply to different cases—that act to later settlements, and to settlements now taking place and likely to take place hereafter. That act was not made to affect settlement rights that had become vested, and would have been void to the extent it would have attempted to do this. Therefore, the nature of this right has got to be considered solely by these early laws alone.

Was it in the power of Congress in 1813 and 1816 to pass a law that, before entry at the Land Office, would invest a settler on public lands, or his assignee, with a vested interest in them?

It was, because the Constitution had invested it with sole and unlimited power on the subject.

It could bind the Government by a conveyance outright, or by a proposition to convey in the future to become binding, when any steps in it provided for acceptance should be commenced to be performed, and by which the Government might from that date stand concluded until a default should be made by the settler, the same as if the proposition had been from the fee owner of wild land to induce some one to improve it.

What is a vested, equitable interest in land? It is an interest which the law protects, and authorizes the owner to transfer to another, and invest the purchaser with all the rights in it, which before sale the settler had.

Did these laws of 1813 and 1816 place such an interest in the settler before the entry of his land at the Land Office? They did, because they protected him from the date of his settlement until all the time given for entry should expire; and, before entry, authorized the settler to sell and transfer all his right and interest, and place the purchaser in his shoes.

The law contained no clause against assignment or transfer before entry, but ran to the settler or his representative, and such a clause in the case of Sawyer *vs.* Pritchett and wife, 19th Wallace, 153, was held to make the word representative mean a purchaser instead of an heir, where there had been a sale; while in the cases of Hughes *vs.* The United States, 4th Wallace, 232, and Bird *vs.* Cravens, 1st Mo., 282, in each case it was distinctly held that a sale of one of these settlement rights before entry invested the purchaser with all the rights of the original settler—all the original settler would have had had he not sold, but entered the land himself. These two last cases arising under this identical law.

These were the only pre-emption laws in force, as before stated, in Illinois Territory prior to 1830. Mr. Scott and Mrs. Clyborne went to Chicago in 1826, and Mr. LeVassar to Illinois Territory, further south, as early as 1817. Each of these witnesses swear that prior to 1830, from the date they first went to Illinois, these rights were sold and transferred before entry, for value paid, like horses or cows, and were regarded as much the private property of the settler as a patent title now is, and that it was understood that when the land should come into the market that the laws of the United States would give them the sole and exclusive right to enter and buy their tract; and Mr. Scott swears these rights sometimes would bring several times as much as would afterwards have to be paid the Government for the land. They were, in fact, as strong an equitable title until default should be made, as a located military land warrant before patent.

How long was this equitable title to last without entry at the land office? Until within two weeks of the time that the tract could be sold at public sale.

What is necessary to do before any tract of land can be sold at public sale? It must have been by the President proclaimed for sale through the Land Department. When was this tract of land proclaimed for public sale? Never. (See statement of case of General Land Office. Such is the fact. The suit hereafter referred to, shows it was not included in proclamation of 1835.)

Then this equitable title is still in full force, and the time to obtain the legal title at $1.25 per acre, as to any land the Government still retains the legal right to, still exists. That is the case. It could not be since, as it has not since been certified back to the Land Department, through which department the proclamation would have to come.

Why don't you go there and get your title, and not bother Congress? Because the land has been taken out of the Land Department by being reserved for military purposes, and that is the only department that, by law was invested, or is now invested, with jurisdiction to hear pre-emption proofs and grant pre-emption certificates of purchase, and it has not been placed back in that department to be disposed of; therefore it has no jurisdiction to sell the land now, and a sale to us now by that department, and even after patent, would leave us just where we are now. It would be void, like the sale of 1835.

As a matter of precaution we shall file our proofs there before the late case there goes up, but shall fear a title allowed by that department for this reason: If this is a reservation it cannot be vacated now by the Land Department making a cancellation or setting aside of the record making the reservation in 1824, for the reason, that all power to do that in the Land Department, and invest that department with jurisdiction to sell, has not resided in the Land Department as respects military reservations since March 3, 1857. We believe Commissioner Williamson was, however, honest in his decision, and with his views, and what was before him, did the only thing he could consistently.

The proof of compliance by said Beaubien with the terms

of these two early laws is this Col. E. D. Taylor, who is generally known throughout Illinois most favorably, testifies that
he was the receiver of the first land office established at Chicago, this being opened in May, 1835, and that when it opened
the said Jean B. Beaubien brought his old friends and
neighbors, who with him offered to swear he purchased a
house on this land in 1812, a house that had been occupied
since an earlier date than 1812, and a piece of ground that
had been cultivated in connection with it prior to that date
by the owner and occupant, and that it had been his house
since 1812, and that from that day, at different times, which
were in 1817 and 1823, he had purchased valuable buildings
on said land that he then still owned, and that both said
register and receiver were thoroughly satisfied that at that
time, that Beaubien had complied with all the requirements
of these early laws of 1813 and April 29, 1816, but not having any blanks, for those laws for either the taking of proofs
or the issuing certificates, and having blanks for the 1834
law, which latter blanks had been furnished from Washington, these being in fact in rotation like checks in a
check book, with ends to each, they used these, supposing
that it would make no difference; and that if any fault is
imputable to any one that the proofs offered under the 1813
law were not taken and a receipt given under that law, it
is imputable to the United States and its agents, and not to
Beaubien, as he did every thing in that respect that could
be done.

John B. Letendre is now 84 years of age nearly, and well
preserved. He is well vouched for as a credible person. He
testifies that in 1815 he was 21 years of age, and worked for
said Beaubien, and boarded in said Beaubien's family in
the year 1815, on this land, at which time there was no building of the Government on this land, these having been
reduced to ashes; and that during 1815 said Beaubien cultivated a piece of ground on this tract of land, and no agent
of the Government was then on it. Letendre did not leave
Chicago until 1836, or later, and much of the time worked

for Beaubien, and states that up to this time this land had remained Beaubien's home. He also states that at that time, in 1815, he learned by common report that Beaubien had then owned that settlement claim for three years, since in 1812.

David McKee testifies, that he went to Chicago in 1822, and that at· that time, that an old house such as has been described, stood on said land, then in use as a stable; that this old house then in use as a stable had, from its appearance, evidently stood there for thirteen or fifteen years or more.

Madore B. Beaubien cannot recollect back further than the spring of 1813, when he was about four years old, having been born in July, 1809.

He testifies that at that time his father had a home on this land and used to visit it yearly, spending a small portion of each year on it, and the balance of his time he was on his business at Milwaukee and Green Bay, all then in Illinois Territory; and that after 1813 his father did not live outside of Illinois Territory, and that, as he then learned and understood from common report, as well as his father, his father had purchased this house in 1812, and from that time regarded it his home.

Beaubien always remained in Illinois, and his family nearly all still reside in Chicago. Beaubien was residing on this tract of land when it is claimed to have been dedicated to Chicago. Hence no question of ignorance of rights arises there.

Mrs. Clyborne and Mr. Scott, of Chicago, went there in 1826, and from and after that date, and previous to 1830, testify that people coming to the country were in the custom of settling down on any unreserved land not occupied by another, and making their improvements, and it was understood that the United States laws would give them a first and exclusive right to buy the tract when it should come into the market. In 1826 Mrs. Clyborne only went through Chicago, stopping over in Chicago one winter, and went down to near what is now Ottawa, Illinois, some eighty miles out of Chicago, where her father two years before had purchased one of these unentered pre-emption rights, moving on to it from Ohio. Both of these witnesses swear that these rights were regarded to be as sacred before entry at the Land Office as patent titles now are, as much private property as a horse or a cow. Up to 1830, it may be said, these early laws were the only laws in force in Illinois. Hence the rights they speak of were, in general, settlement rights, that commenced at a far later date than this of Beaubien's, under the same laws as his.

That there had been an early settlement on this land prior to 1812 is a part of the early history of the northwest, recorded by various writers, and never disputed or questioned; and even if Beaubien had gone on to this land even as late as 1823, as the owner of this original right, it would have been to him equivalent to a residence on this land from as early as 1804, or thereabouts, as these rights by their terms were, before entry, assignable, and invested the assignee with all the rights of the assignor. Hughes *vs.* United States, 4th Wallace, 232; Bird *vs.* Cravens *et al.*, 1st Mo., 282, and 19th Wallace, 153, Sawyer *vs.* Pritchett.

In this last case it was the construction of the same language under a different law. The other cases were under this identical law, and that, in 1823, that none other than Beaubien had any settlement right on this land, will not be questioned. Hence, he was not only the owner of the first, but of all the settlement titles in this fractional quarter section at that time, if the expression is allowable. We much prefer that these affidavits, which are printed in the appendix, shall be read, as an abstract of them does not do them justice. A substantial abreviated statement of these facts has been forwarded by us to the Chicago *Daily Tribune* and to the Chicago *Times*, and are expected to appear Sunday, March 3d, in print in both of them.

If they are not true they can be disproved. We could have cumulated this proof by going several hundreds of miles, to where the witnesses, then boys in Chicago, now live. We did not think it necessary to do this, nor have the means to spare, unless necessary. We can do so still. We believe they will not be questioned.

In the case in 13th Peters, 498, the suit was at law a case of ejectment, which it was known could not be maintained on an equitable title, but as the State statutes of Illinois had provided that a final Land Office certificate should be equivalent to a patent to maintain ejectments, it was hoped to make the certificate that had been issued under the law of June 19, 1834, the basis of recovery, and this law only required possession on the date of the law, June 19, 1834, and to have cultivated some portion of the tract in 1833. The only thing that could avail was to show that the President had not been by law invested with jurisdiction to reserve this land in 1824, and that, therefore, the land was not within the exceptions contained in the law of June 19, 1834, and that by the act of June 26, 1834, and the proclamation for public sale in 1835, not excepting this land, the land had been restored to the jurisdiction, and was then in the jurisdiction of the register and the receiver to sell, and that their sale had passed the land to Beaubien on one of these certificates under which, it was believed by the able counsel in that case, ejectment could be maintained, this being, in fact, so decided by the Supreme Court of Illinois in that very case.

Now while in fact this land, as we think, was erroneously reserved in 1824, as the terms of the 1813 law were more than a license to buy the land in case it should at some time be proclaimed for sale, and in fact guaranteed this right to enter and pay whether the tract should ever or not be proclaimed for sale, and invested the settler before entry with an assignable interest, for which if a note should have been given, it could between the original parties be sued on and a recovery had; and the law impliedly provided that within the given time to enter and buy, the land should not be reserved. (1st Att'y Genl's Opinions, 291.) Nevertheless, the president, having been invested with jurisdiction and power to reserve, and having exercised that jurisdiction by reserving his judgment, though erroneous, he having been invested with jurisdiction to render it, so long as it would stand, would be as conclusive as though the land reserved had been at the time in the occupancy of a settler under the 1841 law. The difference, however, would be that when the reservation in this case should cease, the rights of the settler, and how far vested in this case are to be determined solely by the 1813 law, the law they arose under and the construction that that law had received before and at the time the reservation was made.

Gelpke *vs.* City of Dubuque, 1 Wall., 175, 205.

Chicago *vs.* Sheldon, 9 Wall., 50.

Caldwell *vs.* Carrington, 9 Pet., 86.

As the entry and receipt in that case, which was under the 1834 law, was the sole basis for recovery, no case that could be made by testimony, stipulation, or otherwise, under any other or earlier law could avail, none was attempted. That case was entirely an agreed case, for the sole purpose of trying the virtue of that receipt, and not a single witness in the case was called at any stage, and all the recitals in it are based on the stipulations made to determine the effect of the 1834 entry, the tract not having been subject to entry under the 1834 law; nor would it have then been under the 1813 law, because, still a reservation, it matters not what would have been the effect of an entry then under the 1813 law, which Beaubien had shown himself entitled to had the land then been in the jurisdiction of the register and receiver to dispose of under any law.

That question did not, and could not, until now arise, that the record of reservation is now, for the first, as we believe, to be set aside, and thereby allow the older equitable title still in force in abeyance to revive, and for which the Government is solely trustee of the legal title, and as Beaubien was then the absolute owner of the equitable title, a title that he could then assign and convey and vest the purchaser with all of his rights, and do with it all that he could with a perfected equitable title, that he could then have been invested with by an individual legal owner. The Beaubien rights now are to be determined by the same rule that in such a case would prevail.

We concede that by the entry and receipt of Beaubien under the 1834 law, the subject of controversy in the 13th Peters case, and called in that case Beaubien's purchase, Beaubien acquired no title in law or equity whatever, the entry having been void; that that court was not invested with jurisdiction to hear or determine any other question than under that entry and so-called purchase, and did not attempt to, and had it attempted to, what it would have done would have been a nullity; therefore the case falls back as to what were Beaubien's rights in the land when reserved then in abeyance, and now to revive and be respected. What would they have been if that said purchase had not been attempted, subject to the qualifications that these rights are to be fixed by the 1813 law, as construed prior to 1824, the case of 1st Otto, 330, answers. These rights are not based on any entry, but on this early pre-emption law of Congress, vesting the settler under it with an equitable title in this land from the date of his settlement. No settlement right arises from entry, but solely from the laws of Congress authorizing settlement and entry.

When the reservation of a settler's land is canceled and vacated the settler's right to the land, under the law that right originated under and was created by, revives in full force, the same as if his property had been taken for any other public purpose, and that use had ended. (1st Otto, 330; Shepley et al. vs. Cowan et al.)

But when an old right like this revives it must not only be considered by the old law under which it arose, but by the construction that was given that law at the time. Gelpke vs. City of Dubuque, 1 Wall., 175; Chicago vs. Sheldon, 9th Wall., 50; Caldwell vs. Carrington, 9 Pet., 86.

That law authorized assignment from date of settlement

and before entry, which the 1841 law never has. The 1818 law did not make a note given for one of these rights void, as it is for a right under 1841 law before final and last entry, and final payment. This 1818 law must be given its full efficacy now.

But it is said that this revivor cannot take place in this case for the reason that Beaubien's receipt was canceled by a decree of court, for the reason that it had been issued when his land was not subject to sale by the Land Department. The following is a full record of everything to be found in that case, a case that was commenced before 1839:

[No. 2,710.]

STATE OF ILLINOIS, } ss.
Cook County, City of Chicago,

James W. Brockway, being first duly sworn, makes oath and says that, he is the Recorder of the county aforesaid, and that all the records of the Recorder's office of said county, existing on and before October eighth, eighteen hundred and seventy-one, were, on that day and the succeeding day, destroyed by fire, and that after said fire the constituted authorities of said county purchased and placed in said Recorder's office certain original letter-press copies of abstracts made before said fire by disinterested parties, they being a firm of abstract makers in said City of Chicago, known as Wilmanns & Pasdeloup, which said letter-press copies were placed in said office in the charge of the Recorder, and that certified copies therefrom, under the seal of the Recorder, are used in business transactions in said city and county, and that on pages two hundred and eighty-nine and ninety, in volume number sixteen, of Letter-press Copies of Abstracts of said firm of Wilmanns & Pasdeloup, there appears the following entries which affiant has caused to be copied therefrom in full:

The said entries being as follows, numbered thirty-three (33) and thirty-four (34) of abstract:

[33.]

E. D. Taylor,
  Receiver,
    To
John Baptiste Beaubien. }

Certificate No. 6, dated May 28, 1835, and recorded June 26, 1835, in book D, page 168.—Pre-emption act, 19 June, 1834. Land office at Chicago, Illinois. Acknowledges receipt of $94.61, in full payment for the southwest fractional quarter of section 10, in T. 39 N., of R. 14 E., of 3d P. M., containing 75.69 acres.

[34.]

The United States of America,
    vs.
John B. Beaubien, James Whitlock, Edmund D. Taylor, Sydney Breese, and James M. Strode }

In the Circuit Court of United States for the District of Illinois. In chancery. Bill to set aside the receipt last shown June 13, 1840.

The bill in this cause having been taken *pro confesso* against the defendant James Whitlock, and the other defendants having answered, and the said cause having been brought on to a hearing, &c., and it appearing to the said court that the southwest fractional quarter of section 10, T. 39 N., of R. 14 E., of 3d P. M., situated in the Chicago land district was a military reservation of the United States, and not subject to enter and purchase by the said defendant John B. Beaubien by pre-emption, it is therefore ordered, adjudged, and decreed by the said court, that upon the receiver of the United States Land Office at Chicago refunding or tendering to the said John B. Beaubien the sum of $94.61, being the amount of the purchase money paid by the said John B. Beaubien to Edmund D. Taylor, the then receiver of said Land Office, when the said Beaubien entered the said land on May 28, 1835, as mentioned in the receiver's receipt to said Beaubien, that thereupon said Beaubien deliver and surrender up to the receiver of the Land Office at Chicago, for the purpose of being canceled, the said receiver's receipt so given by him for the purchase money of the said land; and that he also deliver to the said receiver to be canceled, the certificates given by the said James Whitlock and said James M. Strode, as Register of said Land Office, to the said Beaubien, of his, the said Beaubien's entry and purchase of said land; and the said court do further order, adjudge, and decree, that said entry and purchase of the said tract of land by the said John B. Beaubien and the receiver's receipt, and the said register's certificate be vacated, canceled, annulled, and held for nought, and that said John B. Beaubien and the other defendants be restrained and perpetually enjoined from ever setting up or asserting any title or claim to the said land, *by virtue of the said entry and purchase*, and that the defendants pay the costs of this suit.

Affiant further states that the foregoing is the full text of the items, number thirty-three and thirty-four as shown in said abstract, in volume sixteen of said letter-press copies.

JAS. W. BROCKWAY,

Recorder.

Sworn to before me and subscribed in my presence, this 8th day of December, A. D. 1877.

HENRY L. HERTZ,

[SEAL] Notary Public.

STATE OF ILLINOIS, } ss.
Cook County, City of Chicago, }

Samuel Daniels, being first duly sworn, makes oath and says that he has examined the abstract from which the above copies of entries were taken, and that said abstract does not contain any entry or statement pertaining to said suit not above copied and shown; that affiant is one of the deputies of said office to which this matter has been referred, and that affiant does not know of anything in the Recorder's office pertaining to said suit now in existence that will add anything to the information contained in said entries above copied. Affiant has examined about fifteen abstracts of portions of said property this day, and finds nothing in relation to said suit in any or either of them, other or different from that contained in the entries above, or that explains when it was started.

SAMUEL DANIELS.

Subscribed and sworn to before me this 10th day of December, A. D. 1877.

HENRY L. HERTZ,
[SEAL]   Notary Public.

Certificate No. 6—Voucher No. 4.

RECEIVER'S OFFICE,
Chicago, Illinois, December 18, 1840.

Eli S. Prescott, Receiver of Public Money at Chicago, Illinois, has this day refunded to me the sum of $94.61, being the amount paid by me for the southwest fractional section No. 10, in township No. 39 north, range No. 14 east, of the third principal meridian, on the 28th day of May, A. D. 1835.

The entry of said land by myself being invalid, in consequence of its being reserved for military purposes, as per letter from the Commissioner of the General Land Office.

JOHN B. BEAUBIEN.

If this 1835 receipt was void from the time made, the making of it, the cancellation of it, and the return of the money left both Beaubien and the Government as they would have stood if none of these things had occurred. Void conveyances leave grantor and grantee as they would have been without the void conveyance, and where the void conveyance is canceled, and the consideration money returned, prior rights still exist as before.

A pre-emptor's right under this 1813 law, did not and could not arise from an entry under it. Under it like under all other settlement laws, the settler's title arises from the law itself, which is in equity a grant by Congress of the land itself to the settler from the date of settlement, when so provided in the law as was the case here, while the entry is only one of the modes provided to evidence the previous grant. That title existed in Beaubien while none of his land was reserved, and was from the date of its origin the subject of sale, barter or exchange, and protected by law, which are all the privileges pertaining to any property. It was not annihilated by the reservation, but only placed in abeyance and suspense. It is now to revive in Beaubien's heirs in all its original force controled by this 1813 law. (1st Otto, 330.)

The second bar or estoppel alleged is this : That August 1, 1854, Congress simply directed the Land Commissioner to convey to Beaubien nine certain lots that were in equity Beaubien's before the conveyance was made. This direction did not in the act even assume to either give or grant anything to Beaubien, because evidently his before, or require anything to be surrendered by Beaubien not included in these nine lots. The act is in 10th vol. Stat., page 805. Read it. The surveyor sent to Chicago to survey these lots made this report:

"I am requested by Mr. Jean Baptiste Beaubien to state to the Department that he has had assurances from reliable sources that it was the design of the framers of the act for his relief, of August 1, 1854, so to have drawn it as to have given him all the public ground lying south of the line of excavation, except what was reserved for the marine hospital, and the streets provided for in the survey and plat of Mathew Birchard, agent for the War Department, in the year 1839; and Mr. Beaubien, therefore, requests that the said fraction of lot ten of block number two, which lies south of the line, may not be sold or offered for sale until he can have an opportunity of petitioning Congress to pass an explanatory act for his relief on this subject. I beg leave respectfully to recommend his request to your favorable consideration, for the reason that from information I have received from highly respectable sources, I am inclined to think his impressions are well founded."

The following authorities show that Beaubien, by taking these lots, was not estopped from his right to his remaining property: Brooks vs. Haynes, 6th Law Report, Equity (6th,) page 25; Hickox vs. Buckingham et al., 18th Howard et al., 182; Brand vs. Virginia Coal and Iron Co. et al., 3d Otto, 326; Hoffman Coal Co. vs. Cumberland Co., 16th Md., 456; Cumberland Coal Co. vs. Sherman, 30th Barbour, 574.

We have read somewhere in the books that estoppel is odious to equity, and not favored; that it is not presumed, but must be strictly alleged and clearly proved by the party who would avail himself of its protection, and that it is only to be used as an aid and protection to equity, and never to advance wrong; and that it can only prevail when the party against whom it is prayed has not only done wrong, but only where that wrong has been the cause of loss and injury to him who invokes its protection. In summing up this matter we find that the Government has had out of Beaubien's land $272,598, some of which it has enjoyed the use of for thirty-nine years, for which Beaubien has never had any allowance or compensation, and does not ask any. Is this such a monstrous outrage and wrong by Beaubien that he should be estopped from claiming any remaining part of his land from the trustee of his that has thus treated him? If so, then his heirs are estopped from claiming this grant, otherwise not.

Is not this act one of the strongest recognitions of the Beaubien equitable title in this land that the Government could have made?

Could an ordinary trustee make such a conveyance of a part of the trust property, and escape from conveying the balance?

If an executor had held ten blocks in trust, and conveyed one by the same language as the Government used here, he
2

would not have dared to plead estoppel to a bill to compel
a conveyance of the balance; and does not the same rule
that would control the executor, bind the Government here?

It is claimed that Congress by the act of June 24, 1864,
(15 vol. Statutes, 142,) directing the marine hospital at
Chicago to be sold to the highest bidder, thereby confirmed
to the City of Chicago this remaining land of Beaubien's.
It would seem that ratification in this case would be obtained by a very circuitous route, and anomalous law. The
following being, as we have supposed, the law of ratification
where the sale to be ratified was voidable, not void:

"To render the ratification of such a sale effective and
conclusive, the principal must at the time of the ratification
be fully aware of every material fact, and this act of ratification be an independent substantive act, founded on com-
plete information, and he must not only be aware of the
facts, *but apprised of the law as to how these facts would be dealt
with, if brought before a court of equity.*" Hoffman Coal Co.
vs. Cumberland Co., 16th Md., 456; Cumberland Coal Co.
vs. Sherman, 30th Barbour, 574.

The deed which was made by the Secretary of the Treasury in 1872, for the old marine hospital we believe contained
some words and recitals a little broader than this act last
cited, or the act of May 25th, 1872, in reference to this
same matter, by which it is claimed that if no act of Congress had ratified the void sales of the Secretary of War in
1839, that this recital by a department officer of the Government would do it; that such a recital would be an act of
the Government.

We believe it a well settled principle that no officer not
having authority to do a thing can ratify it and make it
binding. · If the recitals of the Secretary of the Treasury in
making this last deed to James F Joy, his authority being
limited, defined by these two last acts of Congress, could
ratify to any person their title to land outside of the marine
hospital grounds, he should while he was at it have fixed
everybody out in the United States, and this would settle that

department officers can act as well without acts of Congress to authorize them as with such acts, and that Congress had best adjourn and go home, and not again meet, as any legislation it may make is unnecessary, and is susceptible of disapprobation by department officers.

It matters not as to whether the sales of 1839 were authorized or not, as to the right of the Beaubien heirs to receive such title as remains in the United States, to the open common between Madison and Randolph street, these streets being considered as extended east to low water mark on the shore of Lake Michigan, for as in 1839 the Government was a trustee for Beaubien for any of the lands in this quarter section, it remained such, and is such now, for any title it retained, which is all the title it now has or can give to any one, and belonging to the Beaubien heirs, she has no discretion but to make the grant to them.

Assuming the dedication to have been valid, it was only for the term that the land should remain vacant of buildings, and no longer. It was not an assurance that after that time the residuary title retained in the Government would also be donated to Chicago. It will be asserted that this residuary title retained has no value, and therefore should be donated. If this be so, why has Chicago labored for years to obtain it from Congress; and if to be donated why shall not the owners be consulted by their trustee before donation is made. Let me suggest to you that there is a rule of law that prevails in Illinois to fix the respective values of such estates, and it is this:

First, what is the land in question worth as an open common? Secondly, what is it worth to do as you please with? The difference of these two values fixes the true and legal value of the estate Chicago now asks as a donation.

Under this rule, if condemnation proceedings are to be had, the Government will receive at least two-thirds of the value of the land in question, as the value of the whole title would be fixed by any jury to condemn, and these proceedings will follow if Congress is firm. As an open common this land is now virtually a nuisance. We shall in a few days have affidavits from reliable real estate agents of Chicago to support these statements, that on this basis the title now asked by Chicago as a donation, has a larger actual value than the other title has which she now claims to own. The adjoining proprietors did not cause the suit in 2d Bissell, 174, to be brought, because they preferred the open space to depot grounds, but as the only means to force the City of Chicago to divide and give to them the one-eighth of what should be received of the proceeds, which by compromise as we are advised by the Chicago press, has since been agreed on between them and the city, when a sale of the property can be perfected. But this land being ours, Congress has no option to either convey to Chicago or retain to be condemned She must convey to the Beaubiens or be a repudiator.

Will a grant to Chicago now aid her one way or another in any controversy with the Valentine scrip hereafter in the courts? Does the value of land have anything to do with the nature of its title; and the setting aside of this land to Chicago, having in fact been a void act, has this land not since remained unappropriated unless held by being reserved or by the Beaubien's equitable title, and has not all the title therein been carried out of the Government by that scrip that was lo table on any vacant unappropriated land, as this in such a case was? And as such location is in fact equivalent to an express grant of the land by boundaries, after a repudiation of the Beaubien title, what would a grant to Chicago now avail?

Much restlessness was exhibited by the Chicago papers why the grant they ask was not consummated at once by Congress, when the recent decision of Commissioner Williamson, holding this land, has passed out of the United States under the Valentine land scrip, was made. If this has occurred, would the prayed for grant to Chicago amount to anything? Is not Chicago in possession, and can she not defend that possession if no title was passed under the Valentine land script, and can she, if the title has passed?

But if the grant is made of the legal title to the Beaubien heirs, they can assert their prior pre-emptive rights in the land that have existed since April 29, 1816, and the Valentine scrip location will pass for nothing, though the land may have been vacant and unappropriated as to all others than the Beaubien interest in it at the time that location was made.

Since the Chicago press has come to understand this they are not as urgent as they were against the Beaubiens.

The Illinois Senators and Representatives were called upon by the Chicago press to vote, and that speedily, this land to Chicago.

It is not necessary to remind these gentlemen that they are acting under the solemnities of an oath, and that this matter between Chicago and the Beaubien heirs is to be determined on its legal merits, the same as though it was a matter between two equally obscure and uninfluential claimants; and is to be determined on the proofs adduced, in legal and proper shape, and not on that of irresponsible newspaper assertions, and on the law applicable to these proofs; and that, judged by this test, the claim of Chicago would not stand a moment with any unbiased mind in Congress or out of it. Her request is not claimed to be based on any legal or even moral right. It is only a petition for charity. The claim of the Beaubiens is that Congress perform a part of its original promise to their father which, in similar cases, since that was made, yes, in over a hundred thousand cases, the Government has performed and recognized thereby that it was both her moral and legal duty to do it, her duty in none of these cases being any more binding than in this.

But it will be said that in these cases the land had not attained so great value as this, nor the right have been so long in force. When was the increased value that had attached to the settlers' lands held a sufficient justification for the Government to repudiate its promise to convey, so long as the settler had not placed himself in default? When was that increased value ever accounted to belong to the

Government, and not to the settler? Does not the same principle and duty govern this case that does that of every settler in the wilds of the West? Did not our father settle here when the nearest post was 180 to 200 miles distant, being Fort Wayne, Mackinaw and Detroit? Was he not in possession and in no default when this land was reserved? Was he not still in possession when this common is claimed to have been set aside to Chicago, and even until the very house the Government had assured him he might die in was by the Government sold over his head, and he compelled to get out of it? Did this inhuman and brutal treatment at the hands of the Government make their duty less now, or in any way impair or destroy the Beaubien rights in land still remaining in the name of the Government? Has it not always been accounted the older the equitable title the better, so long as no default has occurred in it, and the legal title is still in the Government? Must all the rules of law and justice be subverted to rob the Beaubien heirs for the benefit of Chicago?

Chicago is a most inordinate beggar. She begged that this land be left unsold in 1839, for her to enjoy so long as it should remain vacant of buildings. She got this done, and thereby decreased the proceeds of that sale by several thousands of dollars, *as we have the proofs to show.* She claims to have procured nearly a mile front of park lands, by donation from the canal trustees of trust property donated by Congress for a canal; that adjoins this, and is now worth several millions of dollars. Its Court-House square, now worth over a million of dollars, was a donation from the same fund. Also, from this same fund and by a tax laid on the State of Illinois at large, it had a sewer built for it at an expense of two millions five hundred thousand dollars, to bear interest until returned; the State and this canal fund undergoing this expense to drain Chicago, when the official reports of the canal show the canal was serving and could serve all the demands of navigation to be met by the improvement, at an average annual expense of less than ten thousand dollars.

In view of these facts we only suggest that if any more charity is to go to Chicago from the General Government, that it come out of the public treasury, and not from the private estate of the Beaubien heirs.

One of the friends of Chicago has said to us that he has no doubt that Beaubien fully complied with these early pre-emption laws; but intimates that if this be true, and Congress shall grant the Beaubien land to Chicago, the Beaubien heirs, who are very poor, can go into the Chicago courts and sue and recover it.

Our opinion of any person who will entertain such an opinion for a moment is, that he is either an imbecile or a fraud. There is no difference between a trust interest in bonds or a trust interest in lands. The Government is a trustee for the bonds of every National Bank, to secure their circulation. Suppose we suggest that Congress donate the bonds of the Chicago National Banks to the City of Chicago, and then tell the banks they have rights in the courts to recover their property, and sue and get it. Would not the cases be identical?

If the British or any other Government, holding property of any kind in trust for one of our subjects, should knowingly deliver it to another, and then say to our subject we knew at the time it was yours, but thought you could recover it in the courts; unless the property should by that government be returned at once, or atoned for, it would be an act of war, and war would at once follow.

Because our Government is sovereign in itself, and cannot in the nature of things permit any other power to interfere between it and its own citizens in its trust relations with them, it does not assume to use this cloak as a shield to commit piracy on them. It is not supposed to wantonly and knowingly take and convey to strangers trust property as a donation. If a department officer should admit that he had knowingly conveyed the land of a settler to a stranger, it would cost him his position immediately; and it would be such a gross perversion of his trust as to make him personally responsible for any damages that might ensue to the settler.

This case has evidently been referred to have it found if there are any private rights in this land that would make it improper for Congress to convey it to Chicago, and there being such rights, and these also in law and equity being entitled to a conveyance from Congress to their owner, it is trusted that the respective committees of the respective houses of Congress will report against the asked for grant. of Chicago, and in favor of that asked for by the Beaubien heirs, and that Congress will ratify that action by making such grant, so long delayed by the default of the Government.

We are told that in 1839 all the equitable title of this land was placed in Chicago, the legal title being still retained by the United States, and to substantiate this opinion, 2d Bissell, 174, is referred to.

That case decides directly the reverse of this proposition, that decision being that this land was dedicated only so long as it should remain vacant of buildings.

This residuary title we have shown is now worth more, and would be condemned if not given away at a higher price than the title the City of Chicago assumes to have.

But assuming all which that decision claims, that is that on the record made in that case, and the things assumed and conceded by each party to it to be true, that there was such an equitable dedication as has been stated, the legal title still in the Government, would not that legal title exist. in trust solely for the older equitable title, which is the Beaubien title; and in that case could it be to any extent a. trustee to the City of Chicago. Shall the rules of law be subverted in his case, because Chicago has power, wealth, &c., and the Beaubiens are poor and humble?

In regard to the second Bissell case it should be recollected that the Beaubiens were not a party to it, and are not concluded by it, and that all parties concerned in it were interested in showing and making a case of dedication of some kind appear; the purpose of the city being to sell, and gobble all the proceeds; the purpose of those causing the suit to be brought, and using the name of the United States, being to let her sell, when she would make a division with them of what is to be received from the property, which it is understood has been arranged.

There is no legal or moral reason why several hundreds of thousands of. dollars should be given to Chicago, even if the Beaubiens have no equitable right in the land. She did not buy a farthing at the 1839 sale. This space was not left open to enhance the amount received at those sales, nor did it have that effect, but decreased that amount by from $2,000 to $3,000, as no one can dispute who will look at the list of what lots brought fronting this space and near it. compared to other parts, and make any reasonable allowance for what this space would have brought.

This space was left open in violation of the instructions to the agent who sold, and it was hardly thought by the press of Chicago at the time, that it would give any title to the city, but was asked for, nevertheless, on the ground that, whether authorized or not, if left, they would get the benefit all the same.

This agent had also been instructed that if he should not be able to sell the land at Chicago, to adjourn the sale to Detroit or New York—a most remarkable order for a department officer to make, to have the land sold (if necessary to effect a quick sale) at a place a thousand miles distant from the land itself!

The sale had been ordered with all possible dispatch as soon as the case in (13 Peters, 498,) was decided. The people of Chicago on learning of it at once petitioned for delay, for time for Congress to act in the premises, and assigned with other reasons that it was a very bad time to sell, and gave the reasons why it was a bad time, and good reasons too : but the object was to get the land sold as soon as possible, the money into the treasury, and improvements started before Congress could meet to intercept the outrage, hence reasons for delay were needless. This space was left open to reduce the indignation existing in Chicago against the Government for this Beaubien outrage, which at that time hardly had any bounds with party, people or press, and was general thoroughout the west, and justly so too.

The object of this was, that if the land should be certified back to the Land Department as the law required it to be, it would go in the usual order provided by law for sale in that department to the pre-emptor first, at public sale afterwards, and then private sale, and Beaubien would step in and take it, as he could make proof, and would have to pay but $1.25 per acre. This title in Beaubien would have enured back to April 29, 1816, and cut out a late cabinet officer and his friends; therefore such a sale must not be made and was not made.

In conclusion, it being conceded that the legal title of this land is still in the Government, and therefore held in trust solely for the older equitable title, which is the Beaubien title, as well as in trust for any residuary title, which in equity is the Beaubien's also; and it being the promise legal, moral, and equitable duty of the Government to convey to the Beaubiens, and no such duty, promise, or obligation resting on it to convey to Chicago, it is trusted that she will perform this obligation to the Beaubiens; an obligation as sacred in law and honor as any bond ever issued for money borrowed by the Government, and as much within the power of the Government to make when this early law was passed, and no more in its power to repudiate; but if not that she will not convey their property to Chicago, and tell them as their rights are prior to sue, with no money to sue Chicago in the courts and recover it. It would not be a very business-like or honest spectacle for the United States Government to make of itself, notwithstanding it is urged by Chicago's friends. It would not be the law or justice usually meted out to claimants equally poor, obscure and uninfluential, and would be such marked partiality as not to escape the attention of any.

An advocate for Chicago is represented as claiming: first, that because a purchase by Beaubien at the Land Office in 1835, while this land was reserved and not in the jurisdiction of the Land Department to sell, was held to be void, that therefore this is a settlement of what his equitable title would be when the reservation should cease, and the prior equitable right existing in Beaubien before the reservation should revive, which the United States Supreme Court, in 1st Otto, 330, says cuts off all subsequent accruing titles, though a purchase during the time the land was not susceptible of entry would have been void.

The United States Supreme Court in 1st Otto, 330, refers to the cases of Frisbie vs. Whitney, 9th Wallace, and the Yosemite Valley case, 15th Wallace, 77, and then says: "In those cases the Court *only* decided that a party by *mere settlement* upon the public lands, with the intention to obtain the same under the pre-emption laws (of 1841,) did not thereby acquire such a vested interest in the premises as to deprive Congress of the power to dispose of the property; that notwithstanding the settlement Congress could reserve the lands from sale whenever they might be needed for public uses or for arsenals, custom houses, or other public purposes for which real property is required by the Government." * * * * * * * *

" But whilst according to these decisions no vested right as against the United States was acquired until all the prerequisites for the acquisition of a title is complied with, parties may, as against each other, (as between the Beaubiens and Chicago,) acquire a right to be preferred in the purchase, or other acquisition of the land, where the *United States have determined to sell or donate the property.* In all such cases the first in time in the commencement of proceedings for the acquisition of the title, where the same are regularly followed up, is deemed to be first in right.

"So in this case Chartrand, the ancestor, by his previous settlement in 1835, upon the premises in question and residence with his family, *and application to prove his settlement* and enter the land, obtained a better right to the premises under the *law then* existing than that acquired by McPherson by his subsequent State selection in 1849. His right then instituted or initiated could not be prejudiced by the refusal of the local officers to receive his proofs, upon the declaration that the land was then reserved. * * So soon as the claim (of reservation) was held to be invalid to this extent by the decision of this Court in March, 1862, (after thirty-seven years,) the heirs of Chartrand presented *anew* their claims for pre-emption, founded upon the settlement of their ancestor (in 1835.) * * * * · * * * * *

"With the decision declaring the invalidity of this claim to the land in controversy, all obstacles previously interposed to the presentation of the claim of the heirs of Chartrand, and to proofs to establish it, were removed. * *

"It follows that the patent issued by the United States taking effect as of the date of such settlement, (1835,) overrides the patent of the State of Missouri to McPherson, (in 1849,) even admitting that but for the settlement, the land would have been open to selection by the State of Missouri.

If B, owning a residuary title in land, when the present estate and right to present possession rests in A until A shall die, and B, during A's life should bring ejectment against A, would any judgment that could in any court be rendered in such a case preclude B's title after A should die, and B's title come into life? The reservation precluding Beaubien from buying or obtaining his property while it should last has, since 1835, ceased, or is about to, and the Beaubien right to the property come into force, cutting off all subsequently accruing equitable titles.

As the court in the Peters case was not invested with jurisdiction to have passed on Beaubien's residuary title, if it had attempted to, it is a matter of little consequence whether it attempted to or not, but as a matter of fact it did not.

The suit before it was, as before stated, one of law purely, an action of ejectment. No one of legal intelligence ever yet thought of maintaining a suit in ejectment against the Government on an unentered pre-emption right, as all rights that Beaubien then had or might thereafter acquire, under these laws of 1813 and 1816, were at that time, as his entry had been, under the law of June 19, 1834.

What his rights were under this law of June 19, 1834, was all that the court was in that case invested with jurisdiction to hear or determine, or in any way that it attempted to hear or determine. In Illinois then, as yet, the distinction between law and equity prevailed in all the rigor that existed a hundred years ago in England. There was not then, and is not yet, any blending of the two jurisdictions in one and the same suit, or before one and the same court, as now prevails in some of the States having codes.

The claimed law title on which this action of ejectment

was based was a final Land Office certificate under the pre-emption law of June 19, 1834. That law had authorized pre-emptive rights only on tracts that at its date were unreserved, as was by that case decided, which did not and could not have included this, as in 1824 it had been reserved. That act only required the settler to have been in possession on the day this act was passed, to wit, June 19, 1834, and that he should have cultivated some portion thereof in the year 1833—cultivation in any other year than 1833, and residence on any other day than June 19, 1834, to give pre-emptive rights to purchase the tract under the law that entry was based on, would not have been worth a cankered pin or a beggar's sleeve. Nothing else than these sole facts, and whether this land was on the 19th day of June, 1834, reserved, was properly before that court.

No reference was in that case made from beginning to end of the 1813 or 1816 pre-emptive laws for Illinois; no entry having been made under those laws, the case being one of law only. No question arising under these laws of 1813 and 1816, under which we now claim, was or could have been considered in that case.

The case only decided that this purchase under this 1834 law was void, and gave Beaubien no title, and there being before that court no other question that it did or could decide except the effect of this void purchase and entry, it does not in any respect have any effect on what the Beaubien prior equitable title created by the 1813 law, then resting in abeyance and in equity, that could not then be considered in an action of law, and is now to revive, or has revived ; and these rights were entirely unaffected by that decision, save and except as that decision, and the one relating to the cancellation of this entry, conclude the Government from now claiming that this tract of land was included in the proclamation for sale of 1835, and, therefore, that the time for entry by this decision is fixed to not have as yet expired, and, therefore, must now be respected.

That entry and purchase having been void, for the reasons: first, because the land was not at the date of the entry and purchase subject to sale, being then reserved; second, because the land was reserved at the date of the act of June 19, 1834. It left Beaubien's pure, equitable rights in the land the same as though the 1834 law had never been made, or no right had been attempted to be asserted under it. It left this case the same as though after 1824 no attempt had been made by Beaubien to buy under either the 1830 or 1834 law, and this decision had never been made.

Now, an entry before a register and a receiver not authorized by a law of Congress is a nullity. A settler's title, as before stated, comes from the laws of Congress and a settlement under them; and, as before stated, these early laws had provided for this title to exist as sacredly before entry as afterwards, until the time fixed for entry had expired, which has not yet taken place. The entry is only evidence of prior compliance of the settler with the law, and his title never starts from the date of his entry, but from the date of his settlement. This prior equitable title having revived, that in equity passed into our father April 29, 1816, and being now in force and older than all other claimed equitable titles, the Government being a trustee for it alone, we ask to have the land granted to us.

Another point made by our Judge is, that this land has already been confirmed by Congress to Chicago. If so, then what more does Chicago need? And why has she applied for this grant, and why should it be made?

Another point contained in this premature delivery of our Judge, is in substance, that the equitable title of this land passed to Chicago in 1839, but the legal title still remains in the Government. Did Beaubien's settlement begin before or after that date, and was he not then still on this land? Assuming that what you state is true, we would like to know when the Government became a trustee for a second or younger equitable title in lands of which it retains the fee or legal title. Please instance the case.

Do you mean to be understood also that all the equitable title in 1839, or since, has passed to Chicago? Was not that dedication, assuming all that can be claimed for it, limited to the term or period of time that the land should remain vacant of buildings; and has not the time that it can be profitably used in that way already expired? Pray tell. If not, why is a sale being talked of for a depot?

Did Congress receive anything from Chicago in 1839 to leave this open? If so, name the sum. Did she receive more or less than she otherwise would have received from the 1839 sales by leaving it open? Has Chicago received less benefit from this space than the amount she has expended on it? If so, wherein and how? Was not this space left open to appease the indignation of Chicago's citizens against the outrage of that date against Beaubien's rights, and to make it more possible to sell in Chicago, and save the necessity of adjourning and proceeding to Detroit or New York to make the sale? Let the correspondence between Burchard and the Secretary of War answer. Does the bribery fund taken out of what was either Beaubien's or the Government give Chicago any superior equities now? Did not the Chicago press of that date expressly state that they would not pretend to claim this land if it was to be a question between them, and the first, best equitable right of the old settler, Beaubien? Consult the files of the Chicago *Daily American*, now in the possession of the Chicago *Evening Journal*, or come around and read our sworn copies.

If it would have been dishonorable then for Chicago to ask this land, if their asking was to prevent Beaubien getting it, is it any more honorable for her to ask any part of it now, or the Government to donate it, and deny Beaubien's widow and children?

Has Chicago had no aid out of funds provided and set apart by Congress? Let the Canal Fund answer. Is there any reason now why Congress should surrender her title to Chicago, any more than why Chicago should surrender hers to the United States? That is a question for Congress to answer; but as to the Beaubiens, the case is otherwise; as for them, she is a trustee and not an absolute owner in her own right; both at law and equity, as is the case between her and Chicago.

WM. H. STANDISH,

Of Chicago, Attorney for the Beaubien Heirs and Widow.

APPENDIX.

We respectfully call the attention of Congress to the decision of General Williamson, the Commissioner of the General Land Office, in this matter of the application of Thomas B. Valentine to locate this land, as the most able presentation of where this title is, if not in the Beaubien heirs that we have seen, and ask them to read it; but the Beaubiens having an equitable title in it, the Valentine title fails; but unless this land belongs to the Beaubiens, or was a reservation when that scrip was filed, it belongs to that scrip.

AFFIDAVIT OF E. D. TAYLOR.

STATE OF ILLINOIS, } ss.
    County of Cook,

Personally appeared before the undersigned, a notary public within and for said county, E. D. Taylor, who, being first duly sworn, makes oath and says: That he will be seventy-three years of age October eighteenth, eighteen hundred and seventy-seven.

That his memory of past events is strong and clear; that he resides in the City of Chicago and county aforesaid, but spends a good deal of his time at or about Mendota and near Lasalle, Illinois, and that he owns real estate situated in said City of Chicago.

Affiant states that he was the first receiver of the northeastern land district of Illinois, and that his headquarters as such receiver were at Chicago, Illinois, and that the first public sales of any public lands located in what is now Chicago, Illinois, and the country contiguous thereto, commenced at Chicago, Illinois, on the fifteenth day of June, eighteen hundred and thirty-five, and not before that date;

3

and that said lands had not been advertised to be sold before that date at public sale, and that said sales of said lands were made by this affiant as the receiver of the land district aforesaid on and after June fifteenth, eighteen hundred and thirty-five, at Chicago, Illinois, in connection with the register of said land district.

Affiant further states that on the fifth day of February, A. D. one thousand eight hundred and thirteen, the Congress of the United States of America passed a certain act entitled "An act giving the right of pre-emption in the purchase of lands to certain settlers in the Illinois Territory," which act is to be found in the second volume of the United States Statutes-at-Large, on pages 797–798, which act affiant is informed and believes was never repealed, except as it was modified by subsequent legislation on the subject, and that said act is made a part of this affidavit by reference to the same as if incorporated into it verbatim.

That on the twelfth day of April, one thousand eight hundred and fourteen, the aforesaid act, without the change of a word or dot, was extended to a part of the State of Louisiana and to the Territory of Missouri, as will be seen by reference to the United States Statutes-at-Large, volume three, page one hundred and twenty-two. That in eighteen hundred and nineteen in matters that arose in Missouri Territory, that this law was construed by the Attorney General of the United States as creating in the settler from the date of his settlement (where he had settled after the date of the extension of said law to Missouri) a vested right to the tract which he had settled on, which made it impossible for Congress thereafter to reserve it, notwithstanding that at that time no entry of the settlement right had been made at the Land Office, as affiant understands said decision; the same is to be found in the first volume of the Attorney General's Opinions at page two hundred and ninety-one, and to which reference is made.

The time given to the settler under the aforesaid act of February fifth, one thousand eight hundred and thirteen, in which to first enter his land at the Land Office as a claimant under the aforesaid law, did not expire until two weeks before the land was to be offered at public sale, and that within that time for a failure to make entry or the first payment, it was provided in and by said law that the settlers' rights in his land should not be forfeited. The language of said law on this point being in the words following, to wit: " *Provided*, That all lands to be sold under this act shall be entered with the register at least two weeks before the time of the public sales in the district wherein the land lies, and every person having a right of preference in becoming the purchaser of a tract of land who shall fail so to make his entry with the register within the time prescribed, his right shall be forfeited, and the land by him claimed shall be offered at public sale with the other public lands in the district to which it belongs."

Within that time that is more than two weeks before June fifteenth, eighteen hundred and thirty-five, the first time appointed for the public sale of any public lands in Chicago, Illinois, or that were located there. General John Baptiste Beaubien (whose name was sometimes written Jean Baptiste Beaubien, and at others Jean Baptist Beaubien) came to the register and receiver's office of the aforesaid land district then in Chicago, and within two squares of the land hereafter described, and brought with him his neighbors and the oldest settlers then of that locality, and the said Beaubien and these old neighbors and old settlers then and there offered to swear, that for twenty-three years the home of the said Beaubien had been and was then on the southwest fractional quarter of section ten, township, number thirty-nine, north range, fourteen east of the third principal meridian, in the county of Cook and State of Illinois.

The said Beaubien, and the said witnesses by him produced then and there before the said register and receiver, also offered to swear that a house was built on the aforesaid fractional quarter section of land several years before the war of eighteen hundred and twelve, and was occupied up to shortly before the breaking out of said war, and that a piece of ground on said fractional quarter section of land in connection with said house, and by the owner and occupier thereof, was cultivated during each of said years, when the owner and the occupier of said house sold and conveyed the same, together with said cultivated piece of ground, to the said General Beaubien, and placed him in the actual possession thereof, since which time the said General Beaubien had retained said house, and actually lived on said land from year to year and made it his home, and that he actually occupied it before August, eighteen hundred and twelve, in person, and cultivated said piece of ground before that date; that from the last date until the year one thousand eight hundred and nineteen or thereabouts, the said General Beaubien was a fur agent and trader among the Indians, and while this business had caused him to be absent at intervals between those years at Milwaukee and the region of Green Bay, in the former Territory of Illinois, the wife and family of the said General Beaubien had at times during such absence remained on this land to await his return, and that Chicago during that period of time was the home of the said General Beaubien, and that the said General Beaubien offered to swear that he did not establish for himself any other home after the year eighteen hundred and twelve, and these witnesses offered to swear that this was true, and that Chicago was where his wife's relatives had been living during that period, and that it was where she had been reared, and that it was the place said Beaubien became acquainted with her, as was currently understood.

The said Beaubien and the said witnesses also offered to swear that after the spring of eighteen hundred and sixteen said Beaubien had expended for improvements on said lands, over fifteen times the stipulated price the Government had previously offered to receive from him for said lands, any time after their survey, and two weeks or more prior to the time that should be fixed for their sale, and this stipulated purchase price that had been fixed for the sale of said lands to said Beaubien by the Government, to include said expenditures by him on said land, with the necessary and usual proof of compliance with the terms of said law, he then and there tendered to the said register and receiver, and requested them to accept the same and to issue to him the necessary and usual papers, which the Government had promised him, entitling him to a patent for the aforesaid fractional quarter section of land.

At the same time, by the same witness, the said Beaubien offered to prove that he had complied with all of the things required by the pre-emption law of June nineteenth, eighteen hundred and thirty-four, and also tendered his money under that law to said register and receiver for said fractional quarter section of land, and requested that the necessary and usual final papers from said officers be then and there issued to him for the aforesaid fractional quarter section of land. The said register and this affiant then consulted together, and came to the conclusion that the said General Beaubien had complied fully with all of the things that had been prescribed by the said pre-emption law of eighteen hundred and thirteen, and also that he had fully complied with all of the things required by the said pre-emption law of eighteen hundred and thirty-four, but owing to the fact that the Government had some buildings on a portion of said fractional quarter section of land, they deemed it prudent and cautious for them to consult with the authorities at Washington, D. C., before taking any action in the premises, and we made this conclusion known to General Beaubien. Soon General Beaubien, very excited and indignant, came and stated to the said register and this affiant, words to this effect : "See here, my land is advertised for sale ; you are instructed to sell it ; if you take time to write to Washington you will rob me of my land." The said register and receiver then looked at their instructions and found to their satisfaction that what General Beaubien had stated was true. The Department at Washington had seemingly been particular to point out to them every section of land that belonged to the canal trustees, and in which Indian rights existed, and even the land that abutted this piece or fractional quarter section on the west, and also the tract that adjoined it on the south, and had directed all these lands not to be sold, but the said fractional quarter section of land in question it had directed to be offered at public sale unless it should be pre-empted within the time provided by law for pre-emption rights to be entered.

It is affiant's opinion that at that time the pre-emptive rights of the said Beaubien in the said fractional quarter section of land, by the best judges in and about Chicago, were then estimated to be worth not less than fifty thousand dollars, at least they were supposed to be very valuable, and the said register and receiver felt that they had no right to hazard them, and, therefore, they concluded to take legal advice nearer at hand than Washington, D. C. About that time Mr. Baker, the United States District Attorney for Illinois, happened to be in Chicago at the office of the said register and receiver, and they submitted the whole matter to him, turning over to him everything. He made careful examination, read over the law, and took time to consider the matter, when he advised us that both the law and our instructions made it our duty to let General Beaubien pre-empt this land, and that it made no difference to us whether the fort and light-house were on a part of said land or not; that it was our duty to follow the law, whether it hurt or benefited the United States Government, and that the law made it our duty to let said General Beaubien pre-empt this land. Although the said United States District Attorney enjoyed the reputation of being a good lawyer, and it was his duty, as we understood, to advise all United States officials in his district, yet, before acting on his advice, we took that of the Hon. Sidney Breese, who is now one of the Supreme Court Judges of Illinois, and even at that day enjoyed the reputation of being an eminent lawyer.

At about that time he happened to be in Chicago, and at the offices of the said register and receiver, and they submitted everything to him for advice pertaining to the said matter the same as they had to the said United States District Attorney, and they received from him the same advice that they had received from said District Attorney.

Said affiant and said register then concluded to, and did permit, said General John Baptiste Beaubien to pre-empt said fractional quarter section of land. They had blanks that had been furnished them by the Department at Washington, D. C., for the taking of proof, showing a compliance with the pre-emption act of June nineteenth, one thousand eight hundred and thirty-four, and for the certificates to be issued by said register and receiver under said act to the settler, and they had no blanks for use under the said act of February fifth, one thousand eight hundred and thirteen, and they supposed that it made no difference under which of said acts they should take proof; they, therefore, on the twenty-eighth day of May, A. D. eighteen hundred and thirty-five, neglected and declined to take all proof then and there offered by the said Beaubien, showing that he had fully complied with the aforesaid act of February, A. D. one thousand eight hundred and thirteen, and they took proof and issued certificates to said Beaubien for said fractional quarter section of land under the said act of June nineteenth, eighteen hundred and thirty-four, and under said act they accepted payment in full for the aforesaid fractional quarter section of land from the said General Beaubien, and then and there the said fractional quarter section of land was entered on the record books of the said register as sold to the said Beaubien, and receipts were then and there issued and delivered by the said register and receiver to the said Beaubien, of which the following, according to the best of said affiant's recollection, are true copies, to wit:

[No. 6.]   *Pre-emption Act, June 19, 1834:*

LAND OFFICE AT CHICAGO, ILLINOIS,
May 28, 1835.

Received of John Baptist Beaubien, of Cook County, Illinois, the sum of ninety-four dollars and sixty-one cents, being in full payment for the the southwest fractional quarter, of section number ten, in township, number thirty-nine, north of range number fourteen, east of the third principal meridian, containing seventy-five acres and sixty-nine hundredths of an acre, at the rate of $1.25 per acre Bank Mich. paper.

E. D. TAYLOR,
Receiver.

[No. 6.]　　　　　　LAND OFFICE AT CHICAGO, ILLINOIS,
May 28, 1835.

It is hereby certified that in pursuance of law, John Baptiste Beaubien, of Cook County, State of Illinois, on this day purchased of the register of this office the lot or southwest fractional quarter, of section number ten, in township number thirty-nine, north of range fourteen east, containing seventy-five acres and sixty-nine hundredths of an acre at the rate of $1.25 per acre, amounting to $94.61, for which the said John Baptiste Beaubien has made payment in full as required by law.

Now, therefore, be it known that on presentation of this certificate to the Commissioner of the General Land Office, the said John Baptiste Beaubien shall be entitled to a patent for the lot above described.

JAMES WHITLOCK,
Register.

Said affiant further states, that said proof offered that the said Jean Baptiste Beaubien had made his home on this fractional quarter section of land since prior to the war of eighteen hundred and twelve, and had complied with all of the things required by said pre-emption law of eighteen hundred and thirteen, was credited by the said register and said receiver, and that it showed a full and perfect compliance by the said Beaubien with the said act of February fifth, eighteen hundred and thirteen, and also a full compliance with the amendment to said act of April twenty-ninth, eighteen hundred and sixteen, and that said proof was offered within the time required by said acts to have it enure back to the date of the latter act; and that no fault or negligence is imputable to the said Beaubien because it was not taken, but such fault or negligence, if any, rests on the United States Government and on their duly accredited agents, the said register and receiver.

Said affiant further states, that the time for proving up any pre-emption right, if any had existed in any other party to pre-empt said fractional quarter section of land or any portion thereof, expired under the said act of February fifth, eighteen hundred and thirteen, on the first day of June, eighteen hundred and thirty-five; that the said affiant remained as the said receiver in the said Land Office until past the date last stated, and until the land sales that began in said land district, at said Land Office, on the fifteenth day of June, eighteen hundred and thirty-five, were completed, and affiant states that no person other than the said General Beaubien, either before the said first day of June, eighteen hundred and thirty-five or thereafter, made any claim to the said receiver that he had any right to pre-empt the said fractional quarter section of land, or any portion thereof, nor did any person other than the said General Beaubien offer any proof of such a right, or receive from the said receiver a receiver's certificate of pre-emption payment for said land, or any portion thereof.

E. D. TAYLOR.

Sworn to before me and subscribed in my presence, this thirteenth day of September, A. D. 1877.

L. F. CUMMINGS,
[SEAL]   Notary Public.

E. D. Taylor, of Illinois, is an old and greatly esteemed citizen of that State. His statements are entitled to credit.

W. N. MORRISON.

AFFIDAVIT OF DAVID McKEE.

STATE OF ILLINOIS, }
    County of Kane, } *ss.*

David McKee, being first duly sworn, makes oath and says that he is now aged near seventy-eight years, and that he now resides near the City of Aurora, in the aforesaid county, and that in an early day in eighteen hundred and twenty-two, he went to the, now Chicago, Illinois, to reside, and was the blacksmith of the place, and located at or near old Fort Dearborn.

Affiant not then being able to speak the Indian language, did not fully post himself as to who had or had not been living at said place between the year eighteen hundred and twelve and the year eighteen hundred and twenty-two, when affiant first went to said place to live. Affiant, however, does recollect that when he went to said place to live, that there was then still standing east of old Fort Dearborn, south and west of the then Chicago river, an old house then bearing the appearance of having stood there some twelve or fifteen years, or perhaps longer, which old house was then in use as a stable, and from the best information and belief that affiant has, the said old house had then stood on said land that long, and this old house was on the fractional quarter section of land that was east of the now State street in Chicago, and -north of Madison street in said city, and south of the Chicago river.

DAVID McKEE.

Sworn and subscribed to before me this first day of January eighteen hundred and seventy-eight.

LYMAN W. FOSTER,
Notary Public.

[SEAL.]

AFFIDAVIT OF JEAN B. LETENDERE.

STATE OF KANSAS, } ss.
  County of Shawnee, }

Jean B. Letendere, being first duly sworn makes oath and says that he resides near the City of Silver Lake, in said county; that he is over eighty-three years of age, and that from in the fall of eighteen hundred and fifteen until after the year eighteen hundred and thirty-five he resided in and about what is now Chicago, Illinois, and in the fall of eighteen hundred and fifteen affiant entered into the employment of Colonel John B. Beaubien, of that place, and remained in his employment the most of the time until the year eighteen hundred and thirty-six; and that in the fall of eighteen hundred and fifteen, and for years thereafter, affiant boarded much of his time in the family of the said Beaubien, who is now deceased.

Affiant states that at the time in the fall of eighteen hundred and fifteen, that affiant began to work for the said Beaubien, and live in his family; the said Beaubien was then residing in a house near the then ruins of old Fort Dearborn, and near where it was rebuilt about the month of July or August, eighteen hundred and sixteen, the said house being then a few hundred feet east and south of said ruins of a former fort, as it was stated, and on that tract of land which after survey came to be known and described as the south-west fractional quarter of section ten, township number thirty-nine, north range fourteen, east of the third principal meridian, and in the now City of Chicago, County of Cook, and in State of Illinois, and north of what is now, or was when affiant lived in Chicago, known as Madison street, and east of State street and south of the Chicago river.

At the time that affiant entered the employment of the said Beaubien in the year eighteen hundred and fifteen, and then began to board and live in the family of the said Beaubien, then living and residing in a house on said land, affiant learned from the said Beaubien and wife, and from the citizens generally of that neighborhood and vicinity, that the said Beaubien had purchased said house from the rightful owner thereof in the year eighteen hundred and twelve, or at about the time of the breaking out of the then late war; and that the said Beaubien had resided therein a portion of each year since that time, and had each year cultivated a patch of ground for garden, &c., in and around said house, and on said tract of land, and this seemed to be a generally conceded fact in and about that region at that date.

As affiant learned in the same way as he learned about the facts of the purchase of said house, he also learned that the same had first been built about the year eighteen hundred and four, and occupied the most of the time from that date as a private residence, up to eighteen hundred and twelve, as well as since eighteen hundred and twelve, and affiant says that in eighteen hundred and fifteen the said house bore the evidence of age, and looked then as though it had been erected ten or more years previously to the year eighteen hundred and fifteen.

Affiant states that in the same way that he learned the before mentioned facts, he also learned that Jossettie Beaubien, the second and the then wife of the said John B. Beaubien, was at the time the said house had been purchased by the said John B. Beaubien, then living on an adjoining fractional quarter section of land, and that in said neighborhood she had been reared, and that in said neighborhood her family relatives were and had been residing, and for many years thereafter continued to reside, and that the said John B. Beaubien in the year eighteen hundred and twelve purchased said house for a home, and that soon after said purchase his marriage to the said Jossettie Beaubien, whose name before marriage was Jossettie Lafromboise followed, when they went to living in the aforesaid house, and had made the same their home.

Affiant states that from and after the time affiant in the fall of eighteen hundred and fifteen, entered into the employment of the said Beaubien, and began to live in the said

Beaubien's family, the said Beaubien did not during the time affiant was in the employ of the said Beaubien up to and after the year eighteen hundred and thirty-six, abandon the said piece of ground as his home, and that he had a house thereon, and his home thereon on the twenty-ninth day of April, A. D. one thousand eight hundred and sixteen, and that the said Beaubien had as affiant knows of his own personal knowledge, used and cultivated a part of said tract of land in the year eighteen hundred and fifteen, and had in that year resided on the same.

Affiant states that between the years eighteen hundred and fifteen, and the years eighteen hundred and nineteen, the said Beaubien spent a part of his time at Milwaukee, that is near what is now known as Milwaukee, and some of his time at the head of Green Bay, and used to go to Machinaw for supplies; affiant often accompanying him, and sometimes the wife of the said Beaubien accompanied him as far as Milwaukee, awaiting until the said Beaubien was through with his circuit of trip, when she would return with him to what is now said City of Chicago, but that said trips were not made for the purpose of abandoning the home which the said Beaubien had established in Chicago on the aforesaid land, as when absent the said Beaubien and wife always in conversation in the presence of affiant, used to speak of the place on the aforesaid land as their home.

Affiant states that at the time he began to work for the said Beaubien, as aforesaid, in the year eighteen hundred and fifteen, there was no fort or building owned by the Government standing on the aforesaid land, as that term is commonly understood in a new country; that the fort that was said to have been on said land from the year eighteen hundred and four to August, or thereabouts, in the year eighteen hundred and twelve, was said to have been abandoned by the Government at the latter date, and not until after being abandoned to have been destroyed by the Indians of that region, and the said tract of land was then totally abandoned by the Government, and on the twenty-ninth day of April, A. D. eighteen hundred and sixteen, was said to have been then totally abandoned by the United States Government for a period then of near four years, and the war with the British Government had then been ended for the space of about two years, and that it was not then known in the region or vicinity of said land that the Government intended to or ever would resume possession of said land, or any portion thereof, and, as affiant is informed, the said lands had relapsed into the condition of all other public lands, and were then as susceptible to the attaching of pre-emptive rights thereto, under pre-emption legislation and residence on said land, as if the partial appropriation thereof from the years eighteen hundred and four to the month of August, eighteen hundred and twelve, by the United States Government had not existed.

Affiant further states of his own knowledge that about the month of July or August, eighteen hundred and sixteen, and after the twenty-ninth day of April, A. D. one thousand eight hundred and sixteen, the United States Government retook possession of about four acres or less, of what after survey came to be known as a part of the southwest fractional quarter of the aforesaid section of land, and that at said last date there were no surveys in that region, and that the said Government, on retaking possession of this small portion of the aforesaid tract of land, designated the portion it intended to make use of by enclosing the same with a fence, and that said Government fenced off and retained for their use a much larger field on the west of the buildings and small field aforesaid they then used, which larger field was west of what was known as State street, Chicago, Illinois, at the time affiant left said city, and which larger field, west of said State street, was in the fall of eighteen hundred and twenty-four still enclosed by fence, and then known as the Government field, and which in the fall of said last named year, with said small field, was the only land at that date in use by the Government, or known as the Government soldiers land.

Affiant further states that he knows of his own knowledge that in the fall of eighteen hundred and twenty-four, and on the first day of October, of that year, the said John B. Beaubien was then in the actual occupancy, and then actually residing on said tract of land, outside of the said theretofore enclosed and appropriated limits that had been in use by the Government, and that on this portion of said tract of land since, on the twenty-ninth day of April, A. D. one thousand eight hundred and sixteen, the said Beaubien had made for that date, and region, large expenditures for improvements, and which improvements were then still standing on said portion of said tract of land, and still were owned by the said Beaubien, and that they were popularly known as said Beaubien's private property, and that they were then, by the custom and usage of that region, as much an article of sale and purchase, and the title of the settler thereto; as much respected as though the same were his cow or his horse; and, as affiant is informed, the settlement law in force at that date for the territory of Illinois, not only authorized the sale and transfer before entry of such improvements, but also of the guaranteed pereferential right from the Government of the first and exclusive right to purchase the land itself, which right, as affiant is informed and believes, contained the further promise of the Government; that the right of entry and purchase should not be predicated on, whether the land of the settler should ever be proclaimed for sale, and that save and except for a failure of the settler to enter his land within the time fixed by the settlement law his right of entry should not, as affiant is informed, be forfeited by the Government or others.

Affiant further states that he has no interest whatever in who is the owner of any portion of the fractional quarter section of land, first above described, and that he is not an Indian, but a Frenchman, and that he has lived at and near Silver Lake, Shawnee County, Kansas, for twenty-six years, last past; that he has attentively listened to the careful reading of all of the aforesaid affidavit, and fully understands its contents, and that affiant is well and extensively known in the region aforesaid.

JEAN B. LATENDRE, ^{his} ×
^{mark.}

Witness: DR. W. F. HAZELTON.

Sworn and subscribed to before me, and by me read over to affiant before signing, this twenty-first day of December, eighteen hundred and seventy-seven.

WM. F. JOHNSTON,

[SEAL.]   *Notary Public.*

I do solemnly swear that I have known Jean B. Latendre, (whose signature is attached above,) for fifteen years, and know him to be a respectable witness and citizen of Shawnee County, State of Kansas.

W. F. JOHNSTON, *Postmaster,*
Silver Lake, Shawnee County, Kansas.

W. F. Johnston, who is personally known to me, appeared and was duly sworn to the fact set forth in above affidavit, December 21st, 1877.

[SEAL.]   W. F. HAZELTON, *N. P.*

I have been personally acquainted with the above-named W. F. Johnston for twelve years, and know him to be an honorable gentleman in all things, but I have no acquaintance with Jean B. Latendre.

THOS. B. RYAN, *M. C.*

AFFIDAVIT OF MADORE B. BEAUBIEN.

STATE OF KANSAS,   ⎫
County of Shawnee,   ⎬ *ss.*
   City of Silver Lake, ⎭

Madore B. Beaubien, being first duly sworn, makes oath and says that he resides at said town of Silver Lake; that he is past sixty-eight years, of age, and that he was the second son of

Colonel John B. Beaubien, otherwise named Jean B. Beaubien, now deceased; and who was an early pre-emption settler on the southwest fractional quarter of section ten, township thirty-nine, north range fourteen, east of the third prin-
pal meridian in the now City of Chicago, County of Cook,
and State of Illinois.

Affiant states that his memory of the matters hereafter
stated runs back to the spring of eighteen hundred and thirteen, and these matters and things herein stated as having
occurred prior to that date are based on such information as
affiant, after the spring of eighteen hundred and thirteen,
obtained from his father and from his stepmother, Josettie
Beaubien and the other people then living in and near the
aforesaid fractional quarter section of land, and are true according to such knowledge and the best of said affiant's belief.

With this qualification affiant states that in the year eighteen hundred and twelve the father of affiant purchased from
the rightful owner thereof a dwelling-house on the aforesaid
fractional quarter section of land that had been built thereon
about the year eighteen hundred and four, and used and occupied from and after the year eighteen hundred and four,
and from and after said last date a piece of ground on said
fractional quarter section of land, and in and about said house
by the rightful owner and occupier of said house had from
year to year been cultivated.

Affiant personally recollects that early in the year eighteen
hundred and thirteen the father of affiant, and with affiant,
and with the stepmother of affiant, and then the wife of the
father of affiant, were all residing in the said house on
said tract of land, that, as before stated, had been purchased by him during the year eighteen hundred and
twelve, and that each year thereafter the said John B. Beaubien occupied said house and land a portion of each year,
and at all times from and after that date spoke of the same
as their home, even when absent from it; that in eighteen
hundred and seventeen, or thereabouts, the said John B.

Beaubien purchased another house on said tract of land of one Dean, and from and after that date during his yearly stays at the now Chicago, Illinois, ceased to occupy and use the aforesaid house that had been built about eighteen hundred and four, and purchased by him in eighteen hundred and twelve; and the said first house was turned into a stable or barn, and from and after eighteen hundred and seventeen or thereabouts was so used.

Affiant states that when the said John B. Beaubien in eighteen hundred and twelve, purchased his said first house on said land, that he was then about to marry, and soon did marry Jossettie Lafromboise, who had been reared in that locality, and whose relatives then resided there, and that she was then residing on an adjoining fractional quarter section of land, and that the said purchase was made for the his permanent and future home, that the said marriage was made, and the said Gen. John B. Beaubien and wife remained residents of Chicago, aforesaid, on the aforesaid land, until after eighteen hundred and thirty-nine, on which tract of land there was born unto them as the fruit of said marriage a very large family of children.

The business of the said John B. Beaubien did not permit him to be permanently located at any one point for a whole year. He was then an Indian trader, and was required to be some of the time in each year at the now Chicago, Illinois, some of the time at the now Milwaukee, Wisconsin, and some of the time at the now Green Bay, Wisconsin, all of which points at that time and for years thereafter were in the then Territory of Illinois, but that the said John B. Beaubien never at any time in his life resided or did business at Mackinaw, save and except as he visited that point to take his furs, and purchase his supplies for use at the aforesaid posts in the then Territoy of Illinois.

On these trips to these posts in the then territory of Illinois the wife and children of the said John B. Beaubien, from 1812 to 1819 or thereabouts, usually accompanied him, going by way of boat; and particularly was this the case as to his trips to the now Milwaukee and Chicago, as these points were quite near each other, and by a water route connected. These trips to the north by the said Beaubien were, however, for business purposes solely; and as soon as that business necessity ended the said Beaubien settled down and remained permanently on the aforesaid tract of land in Chicago, and during absence on these northern trips the said John B. Beaubien and wife always used to speak of the said Chicago place as their home; and at none of said northern posts during the continuance of these trips, or the time they were being made, did the said John B. Beaubien make any such purchases as the said Dean purchase, or the eighteen hundred and twelve purchase of improvements on the aforesaid tract of land, so far as affiant is informed; and had such purchases been made at these northern posts affiant believes he would have known of them.

Affiant states that from and after the time his father purchased said house on said tract of land in the year eighteen hundred and twelve, that he did not remove at any time thereafter, in any period of his life from the then Territory of Illinois, and that on the fifth day of February, A. D. one thousand eight hundred and thirteen, the said tract of land was not in the occupancy and use of the United States Government for any purpose whatever, and therefore as affiant is informed and believes was not a reservation by occupancy, and that at said date no part of said tract of land had been entered as reserved at any Government land or other office, as affiant is informed and believes, that the said tract of land was not then a reservation for any purpose either by occupancy or entry, and that no part of said tract of land was at that date reserved from sale by any act of Congress, nor had any part thereof been directed to be sold in town lots or out lots, and therefore that as said affiant is informed, the said tract of land became and was subject to the attachment of pre-emptive rights thereto by settlement, theretofore made, or thereafter to be made on said tract of land, under the provisions of the pre-emption law of the above date, for the then Illinois Territory, with the exception, that the aforesaid tract of land on survey might be found to be a fractional quarter section of land, and held to be excluded for that reason from the pre-emption settlement, and that to meet such a contingency and other contingencies, affiant states that an amendment to said act was passed and approved, April twenty-ninth, eighteen hundred and sixteen, making the said law applicable to fractional quarter sections of land, and that on the date of the passage of this amendment the said tract of land had not in any way been in the occupation or use of the Government for nearly four years, either by an agent in possession, nor did it have a building thereon, or a fort thereon of the Government, nor had it had for the space of about four years, and the said John B. Beaubien was then in the actual possession of said tract of land with a house thereon, and had had possession thereof and cultivated a portion thereof for several years, and at said date the Government had not been in possession of any part of said tract of land for a period of near four years, nor was it known in the vicinity of said land at that time, that the Government ever intended to resume possession of any portion of said tract of land, nor at said last named date, so far as affiant is informed and believes had any portion of said tract of land been reserved by any former act of Congress, or directed to be sold in town lots or out lots.

Affiant further states that after this tract had thus passed in equity to the said John B. Beaubien, under and by virtue of the said legislation of Congress, giving him a pre-emption right therein, one of the officers of said Government with a company of its troops, in the month of July, or thereabouts, of the year eighteen hundred and sixteen, took possession of about four acres thereof, and enclosed the same by a fence, thereby designating the extent of the land thus appropriated, and erected a Government building inside of said fence, which post so fenced and enclosed was not at the time known would include any of the land, which by an equitable grant from Congress had previously passed to, and become vested in equity in the said Beaubien, as it was found when the said tract came to be first surveyed by the Government of the United States, which said first survey was not made until about the year eighteen hundred and twenty-one, as affiant is informed and believes, and that, as affiant is informed and believes, the land in said tract or fractional quarter section of land, not in July, eighteen hundred and sixteen, for the use of the Government, taken possession of would have remained, by the terms of the said two pre-emption acts, subject to pre-emption settlement after that date, had the same not before that date been settled on and been then owned by the said John B. Beaubien, and affiant states that on the said part of said tract, or fractional quarter section of land, outside of the enclosed limits of said fort, rebuilt in eighteen hundred and sixteen, were both the houses and cultivated piece of ground purchased by said Beaubien in the year eighteen hundred and twelve, and the house, that in or about the year eighteen hundred and seventeen the said Beaubien had purchased of one Dean, this Dean house being then comparatively new, and for that date of much value, and the said part of said tract of land that was outside of the post limits had been, and was the home and residence of the said John B. Beaubien at the time said tract of land was first surveyed, and at the time the survey and plat thereof was filed and approved in the proper office therefor, and the said Beaubien was also in the possession and actual occupancy of the said land on the first day of October, eighteen hundred and twenty-four, and then had valuable buildings thereon, procured at his own private expense, and then regarded his private property, at which latter date, as affiant is informed and believes, the said buildings of the said Beaubien, and his said land were, without his knowledge or authority therefor, reserved for the use of the General Government without any compensation therefor being made to him, the said Beaubien, and that from and after said last named date, the said tract of land remained reserved for the use of the Government until the spring of eighteen hundred and thirty-nine, and that a part of said tract of land did not cease to be such a reservation until on or about the twenty-fifth day of May, A. D. eighteen hundred and seventy-two.

Affiant states that he has read the said acts of February fifth, eighteen hundred and thirteen, and the amendment thereof, dated and approved April twenty-ninth, eighteen hundred and sixteen, and that he is familiar with what the said John B. Beaubien did in compliance with the terms of the said acts, and he states that at the time of the said appropriation of about four acres of said tract or fractional quarter section of land by the Government of the United States, the said Beaubien was in no default with any of the terms of either of said acts, and was then in the actual possession of said tract of land; and that when a reservation of the residue of said tract or fractional quarter section of land was made by entry in the Land Office on the first day of October, A. D. eighteen hundred and twenty-four; that the said John B. Beaubien was then in no default with any of the terms of either of said acts; and that on said last date, as before stated, the said John B. Beaubien was also in the possession of said tract of land then residing thereon.

Affiant further states that he is advised and believes that the said reservation, notwithstanding the said private rights theretofore and then in said land in favor of the said John B. Beaubien operated to exclude the said land from either entry or sale until it should cease to be used by the United States Government, and the reservation of the same entered in the Land Office, should be canceled and vacated; and that while this reservation should last the pre-emption right of the said Beaubien could not in any way be asserted; and that if he should attempt to assert it his act, whatever it might be, would be void; but that nevertheless his pre-emption right for the period of time the reservation would last would continue to exist in abeyance in the land to revive upon the reservation being vacated.

Affiant states that he is advised, and believes, that the said reservation as to a part of said tract of land was first vacated in the spring of the year eighteen hundred and thirty-nine, by the issuing of an order for the sale thereof; and that the said order was then made by the Secretary of War that he, as Secretary of War, would cause the same to be sold, after being subdivided into lots and blocks, and be sold in single lots to the highest private bidder, and not otherwise, which lots were of about the size of twenty-two feet front by usual and ordinary depth for city lots to alleys in the rear, and some perhaps a little larger; that the manner and terms of said order were of themselves a prohibition to the said John B. Beaubien; that the said tract would not in whole or in any part be sold to him as a pre-emptor; and that being ordered to be sold by the Secretary of War, the said order was a refusal to give the said John B. Beaubien the privilege to first prove and enter and purchase the same, as the law, as affiant is advised, required, for the reason that at that time the said Secretary had no authority or jurisdiction, nor has he ever had, so far as affiant is informed, to hear and determine pre-emptive proofs, or to issue and deliver pre-emption certificates of purchase; nevertheless, affiant states that the said John B. Beaubien was then ready and anxious and able to make the necessary proof of his settlement on the aforesaid tract of land, and of his compliance with the requirements of the aforesaid pre-emption acts; and that the said John B. Beaubien was then in the actual possession of said tract of land, residing thereon, and that the said Beaubien and his heirs have always been ready and anxious to make the proper proof, entry and payment for said land under said law, and that they are still ready and prepared to do this, but that no hour or moment has, that affiant is aware of, ever been allotted them to make this proof, entry, and payment since the aforesaid tract of land was reserved, as aforesaid, and while the said pre-emption title of said John B. Beaubien was in full force, and before he had made any default.

Affiant further states that the said early laws are, as he is advised, still in full force as to said early settlement, and unrepealed, and that the time allotted by them for preemptive proof, entry, and payment of said tract of land has not as yet expired, and that quite a large tract of said land now claimed by the city of Chicago still remains as an open common, unsold and unconveyed, with the legal title still in the United States Government, and subject to the trust in favor of the said Beaubien and his heirs that existed on the days that it was appropriated and reserved, as aforesaid, as affiant is informed and believes; and that the heirs of the said John B. Beaubien, nearly all of whom still reside in the city of Chicago, Illinois, aforesaid, are now ready and willing and anxious, as they have been at all times heretofore, to tender proof of compliance with said law by their father, and to offer and pay the sum of one dollar and twenty-five cents per acre, fixed by a solemn act of Congress as the price to be paid therefor, to induce the said John B. Beaubien to remain on said tract of land and make large expenditures thereon for buildings, while the same was unreserved and unappropriated, and which in fact had that effect and operation.

Affiant further states that in addition to the aforesaid act of estoppel as against the United States Government, to make good their solemn and written promise to convey to the said Beaubien and his heirs the said tract of land, or any remaining part thereof at the price aforesaid, before they would permit it to be sold, granted or conveyed to others, that the said United States Government, in and by the said pioneer residence of the said John B. Beaubien, received a great reward and benefit from the said John B. Beaubien in this. That he came to said locality when the United States was unable or failing to maintain a suitable force in that locality to cope with the then powerful tribe of Pottawatamie Indians, then inhabiting the country in and about the now City of Chicago, and when the garrison of troops there had all been murdered, and the white settlers had been or were compelled to flee for their lives, and remain absent for the space of about four years. This tribe of Indians at this time were wholly under the control of the British Government, and during our then war with that power their fast allies, and such agents and persons, as the United States Government had sent in among them, to prevent and break up this alliance had been unavailing, and it was necessary and desirable to the United States Government for some one to go and be with them that could and would materially aid in this task. The said John B. Beaubien being an American citizen by birth and education, and then and at all other times truly and thoroughly loyal to the United States Government, and having been born and reared in the now City of Detroit, Michigan, and surrounded with Indians from the time of his birth, and fully understanding their character, and in a large measure enjoying their confidence, did at this critical time marry Josettie Lafromboise, then one of the said tribe of Indians necessary to be conciliated, and through her and her family, who were very influential members of said tribe of Indians, and then somewhat more enlightened than the generality of the other members of said tribe of Indians, the said Beaubien did all in his power without any fee or reward, to bring about this reconciliation of these Indians to the United States Government, and in this he was aided by his wife the mother of the larger part of the now Beaubien children and heirs, claiming title to the aforesaid tract of land, the desired result was secured, and the said Indians after that war became the most loyal to the United States Government, and instead of being a great menace to pioneer settlement, became a strong police force to aid in their protection, and in the Indian war that occurred in that region, or west of there, in the year eighteen hundred and thirty-two, these Indians rendered meritorious service in aiding the United States Government to suppress it, and from and since that date it is believed by affiant that they have been truly loyal, and well disposed to the United States Government, and all its citizens and subjects.

Affiant further states that not desiring to rest his father's loyalty and the value of his said services on the testimony of a son, he takes occasion and does refer, for further proof of these qualities in affiant's father to the resolutions adopted at an indignation meeting held by the citizens of Chicago, Illinois, on the — day of June, 1839, on the occasion of the Government of the United States, through an alleged agent of the then Secretary of War, causing the said land so promised as aforesaid many years theretofore by Congress to the said John B. Beaubien by a solemn law to then in repudiation of said law and promise to be subdivided as aforesaid into little lots of about twenty-two feet front, and to be sold to the highest bidder, and the proceeds placed in the United States Treasury, under which, with other parts of the said land of the said John B. Beaubien as the said alleged agent of the then Secretary of War, had caused them to be sold away from the said John B. Beaubien the very house that then in his old age he was inhabiting, and in which he had resided in since Illinois was a Territory, and which house had been procured at great expense to the said Beaubien, and in which a large family of children had been born unto him and partly reared; and in and around which house on the said land so sold and conveyed were also the graves of the departed children of the said Beaubien.

Affiant states that the resolutions of said meeting, which were printed in all the city papers of Chicago aforesaid at the time, and which are still in existence, did not overdraw ·the picture as to what the said Beaubien had done for said locality and the United States Government; but affiant knows as a fact that they left many things in the favor of the said Beaubien unsaid which might have been said. .

Affiant further states in explanation of the letters of Dr. Wolcott, written from Chicago to the Department at Washington, D. C., advising a reservation to be made of the aforesaid fractional quarter section of land for the uses of the Government, and that a larger tract than the whole of said fractional quarter section of land was then under fence and in the

use of the Government, or language to that effect; that the
larger part of the land thus referred to was outside of the said
fractional quarter section of land, and in section nine in the
aforesaid township, and that in the said Beaubien fractional
quarter section there was then only about four acres inclosed
and in the use of the Government, or that at any time since
the retaking possession thereof in 1816, had been in the use
of the Government, and that the part of the said Beaubien
fractional quarter section then in use or inclosed by the Government is correctly represented by the western inclosure
shown in a picture of Chicago in the year eighteen hundred
and twenty, which picture was shortly since shown affiant by
William H. Standish, Esq., of Chicago, Illinois, with the word
"Childs" printed on it, while the eastern enclosure shown
on said picture shows houses and buildings then owned by
the said John B. Beaubien, and to show the field above
referred to in section nine of said township that had been
fenced in and used by the Government to raise vegetables,
&c., for the soldiers at the post. The said affiant has caused
the following map to be drawn:

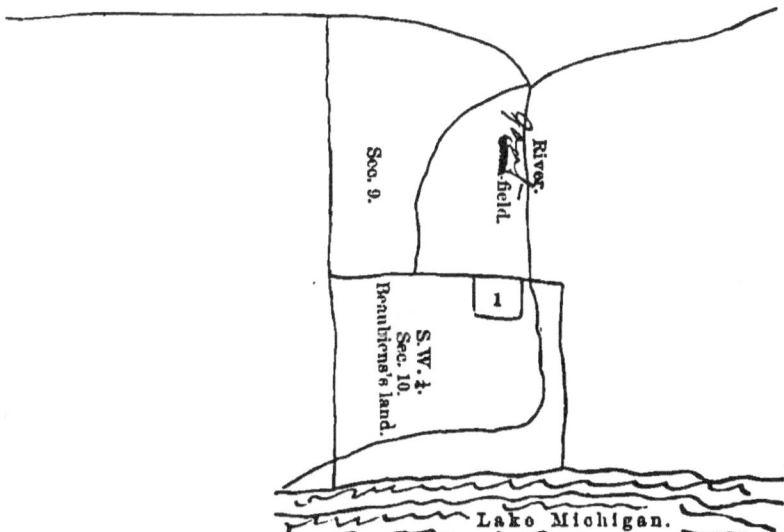

EXPLANATIONS.—No. 1 is fort and enclosure on the Beaubien tract of land.
The other enclosure is west of the Beaubien tract of land.

Affiant states that he was residing at the city of Chicago aforesaid when that part of the reservation by occupancy aforesaid that had been made in July, 1816, or thereabouts, and after survey was found to be in section nine aforesaid, was vacated and ceased to be used by the soldiers at Fort Dearborn, and until after the sale and disposition thereof was made and affiant states that the part of said reservation in existence by occupancy, on the third day of March, eighteen hundred and nineteen, situated in said section nine upon becoming after that date vacated, was permitted to and did relapse back into the condition of public lands that had never been appropriated or reserved, and was sold and disposed of in the same manner as the other public lands in and about Chicago aforesaid that had never been sold or appropriated prior to the grant to the State of Illinois for canal purposes, and said field was not sub-divided, sold or disposed of by the Secretary of War, notwithstanding that the said lands were sold and disposed of between the years eighteen hundred and nineteen and eighteen hundred and fifty-seven by grant of public lands to the State of Illinois.

Affiant further states that at the time a subdivision of the aforesaid tract of land known as Fort Dearborn Addition to Chicago, Illinois, was made, platted, and filed of record, and at the time all the Fort Dearborn sale of lots out of said tract, in the year eighteen hundred and thirty-nine, was made, and at the time the City of Chicago took possession of a part of said tract of land that at said sale was not sold, · the said John B. Beaubien was in the actual possession of said tract of land, residing thereon with his family, and the said City of Chicago, and all parties concerned, had full notice of all his rights in said tract of land, and as affiant is informed and believes, that before said alleged sale, and while it was progressing, they were publicly notified by one of the then able and noted lawyers of Chicago that said sale would be invalid and convey no title to a purchaser thereat.

Affiant further states that the said John B. Beaubien was

in the actual possession of said fractional quarter section of land on the twenty-ninth day of May, A. D. eighteen hundred and thirty, and that he cultivated a portion of said tract of land in the year eighteen hundred and twenty-nine.

Affiant further states that the said John B. Beaubien was in the actual possession of said fractional quarter section of land on the nineteenth day of June, A. D. eighteen hundred and thirty-four, and that he cultivated a portion thereof in the year eighteen hundred and thirty-three.

Affiant further states that that part of the aforesaid fractional quarter section of land now claimed by the City of Chicago, and that other part known as the railroad grounds, were neither to any extent in the occupancy and use of the United States Government, on and prior to the first day of October, A. D. eighteen hundred and twenty-four, for any purpose whatever, and as before stated as affiant is informed no part of said parts of said fractional quarter section of land were, until October first, eighteen hundred and twenty-four, reserved in any way by the Government of the United States, and further affiant saith not.

MADORE B. BEAUBIEN.

Sworn and subscribed to before me the 28th day of January, A. D. eighteen hundred and seventy-eight.

JOSEPH B. OLIVER,
[SEAL.] Notary Public.

WASHINGTON, D. C., February 6, 1878.

I have been personally and well acquainted with Madore B. Beaubien during the last past twelve years, and I regard him as a most upright, honest and truthful man.

THOS. RYAN, M. C.,
3d Kansas.

AFFIDAVIT OF WILLIS SCOTT.

STATE OF ILLINOIS, }
  County of Cook, } ss.
  City of Chicago. }

Willis Scott, being first duly sworn, makes oath and says that he now resides in said city at the northeast corner of Green and Washington streets; and that he came to said Chicago to reside in the year eighteen hundred and twenty-six; and that since that date he has resided at said Chicago, and in northeastern Illinois, contiguous to said Chicago.

Affiant states that when he came to Chicago aforesaid to reside in the year eighteen hundred and twenty-six, and during each year thereafter prior to the year eighteen hundred and thirty, as well as after the year eighteen hundred and thirty, it was the custom of the settlers to select a piece of government land and settle down on it and improve it, and where the land had not been surveyed so as to mark the lines of quarter sections and of fractional sections, the settlers on the prairie used to plow a furrow to mark their boundaries, and in the timber they used to mark and blaze their timber, and what would be found inside of these lines was understood to be the settlers lands, commonly called his settlement claim.

These titles by the settlers were regarded as sacred as the land and home of any man now who has his deed, and the settlers evinced the same interest in building on and improving their claims as though they then had their patent from the Government, as it was understood that after survey, and before the time for public sale by the Government, the settler would have the first and best right to enter at the Government Land Office and buy his claim or tract to the extent of one quarter section of one hundred and sixty acres, as the boundaries should be fixed by survey and made to in-include his improvements and buildings; and prior to this time of such entry and purchase at the Land Office these settler or pre-emption rights were sold and exchanged, and were regarded as much as a sacred right and the private property of the settlers as though the same were his horse or his cow.

Affiant, however, is not aware that any of these claims in and about Chicago aforesaid were entered at any Government Land Office until after the year eighteen hundred and thirty, and thinks that they were not so entered, as it was then understood that the settler would have until the time his tract would be proclaimed for sale in which to enter and purchase his land as a pre-emption settler; and so far as affiant is informed and believes none of the lands in and about Chicago of the General Government were proclaimed for general sale until about the year eighteen hundred and thirty-five, when the Chicago Land Office was first established, and then it was that many of the old settlers first entered their claims and obtained their Land Office certificates. These claims sometimes used to sell before entry for quite large sums of money; many times more than the Government price.

WILLIS SCOTT.

Sworn and subscribed to before me, this twelfth day of January, A. D. 1878, at the city and county aforesaid.

C. R. MATSON,

[SEAL.] *Notary Public.*

STATE OF ILLINOIS, } *ss.*
Cook County, City of Chicago. }

Mary Clyborne being first duly sworn, makes oath and says that she is the widow of the late Archibald Clyborne, of the city of Chicago aforesaid, now deceased. That she was the daughter of James Galloway, formerly of Ohio, near Sandusky. That in the year eighteen hundred and twenty-four the father of affiant left his said home in Ohio near Sandusky and came out to Illinois, and returned to his home in Ohio in May, eighteen hundred and twenty-five, and on his return reported to his family that he had bought out a settler's right in Illinois, near what is now known as Marsailles, Illinois, a town about eight miles from what is now Ottawa, Illinois.

In the year eighteen hundred and twenty-six affiant's father removed his family, including affiant, from Ohio, and wintered over that winter in Chicago, Illinois, and arrived the next spring at the claim he had purchased on his trip three years before, and from that time until in the year eighteen hundred and twenty-nine, affiant lived on the land her father had purchased in eighteen hundred and twenty-four or eighteen hundred and twenty-five as aforesaid, the claim or right as affiant understood, being a legal right in the land given by law, to hold and control it until it would be surveyed and come into the market by the Government, when it was stated and understood the settler within this time would have the right to enter his land at the land office and purchase it at one dollar and twenty-five cents per acre. These were the only titles then known in any part of that region of country; they were bought and sold among the settlers, and were regarded as the private property of the first settler, or of those who had purchased from him, and were deemed as sacred as their horses or their cows, and the most of these settlements were stated to be new.

In the year eighteen hundred and twenty-nine, when affiant married and removed to Chicago aforesaid, there had been no entry at the land office of the United States by the settlers of that region, nor by said affiant's father.

Affiant however learned from her father that after his removal to Chicago, aforesaid, he entered and purchased his claim of the Government as a pre-emption settler, but whether he made his entry and proof under a law passed in eighteen hundred and thirty, or a later law, or under a law passed prior to the year eighteen hundred and thirty, affiant does not know.

Affiant now resides at number six hundred and fifty-two Elstern avenue in Chicago, aforesaid.

MARY CLYBOURN _{her} ⋈ _{mark}

Sworn and subscribed to before me this 24th day of January, A. D. eighteen hundred and seventy-eight.

HORATIO HILL,
[SEAL]   *Notary Public*,
From January 5, 1875, to January 5, 1879.

The words "the next spring," and "on his trip ten years before" on first page, and the words "of" and "were" on second page interlined before signing.

MARY CLYBOURN.
Attest:
HORATIO HILL,
[SEAL.]   *Notary Public.*

STATE OF ILLINOIS, ⎰ *ss.*
   Cook County, ⎱

John Bates, being first duly sworn, makes oath and says, that he now resides in the aforesaid city, at 74 Van Buren street, and that he has resided in said city since the year eighteen hundred and thirty-two; and that from that time to this he has been acquainted with the condition of the so-called Lake Front in said city, in the southwest fractional quarter of section ten, town thirty-nine north, of range fourteen east of the third principal meridian, and between Randolph and Madison streets, and that he verily believes that said city has received more revenue for its use than it ever expended thereon, aside from the use it has had of it as a park.

JOHN BATES.

Sworn and subscribed to before me, this 5th day of February, A. D. 1874.

D. F. FLANNERY,
[SEAL.]   *Notary Public.*

We have an affidavit of James Appleton, of Chicago, who has resided there since 1842, to the same effect as the above, and can pile this class of affidavits mountain high.

Hon. J. A. WILLIAMSON,
    Commissioner of the General Land Office,
        Washington, D. C.

DEAR SIR: Assuming that the proclamation for the public sales of public lands that took place in Chicago, Illinois, in June, 1835, did not include the southwest fractional quarter of section number ten, town thirty-nine north, of range fourteen east, of the third principal meredian, in the now City of Chicago, County of Cook, and State of Illinois, as was decided by the court to be the case, has this tract ever yet been proclaimed for public sale. If so, when? State what the showing of the records of your Department are on this point.

Yours, respectfully,

W. H. STANDISH.

MARCH 6, 1878.

[No. 24,638.]
DEPARTMENT OF THE INTERIOR,
    GENERAL LAND OFFICE,
        WASHINGTON, D. C., *March 7th*, 1878.

W. H. STANDISH, ESQ.,
    Washington, D. C.

SIR: Your letter of the 6th instant, asking if the southwest fractional quarter section ten, township thirty-nine north, range fourteen east, of third principal meridian, Illinois, was ever proclaimed, has been received.

In reply I have to state that it appears from a letter of this office, to Hon. J. C. Calhoun, of the 1st October; 1824, that fractional section ten, said town, and range, was reserved for military purposes. The tract however does not appear to have been expressly excepted in the proclamation of February 12th, 1835, embracing said township, which was offered June 15th, 1835. No proclamation embracing said township subsequent to the above appears on the tract book of this office.

Very respectfully,

J. A. WILLIAMSON,
    Commissioner.

The court in 13th Peters, 498 case says : " But we go further and say that wheresoever a tract of land shall have once been legally appropriated to any purpose, from that moment the land thus appropriated becomes severed from the mass of public lands, and that no subsequent law or proclamation or sale, would be construed to embrace it, or to operate upon it, although no reservation were made of it." Argument then follows to illustrate this, with a conclusion that this tract of land was neither included in the 1834 law, or the February 12th 1835, proclamation for sale, while in the case in which the record is given on the thirteenth page of this brief, between Beaubien and the Government, this point was expressly decided as to this tract, that it had not, in 1835, been in the jurisdiction of the register and the receiver to sell, being then reserved.

This tract not having been purchased in 1835, nor since, it has never been proclaimed, and therefore the time for the pre-emption entry by Beaubien or his representatives has not expired; and they still remain in Illinois, and are ready and prepared, and now offer to enter and purchase the land described in these bills in the House and the Senate.